Other Books by

Playing for Real: Exploring Child Therapy and the Inner Worlds of Children (Basil)

"[His] understand[ing of] the emotional turmoil of troubled children... sets an extraordinary standard." —*Kirkus Reviews*

"Will complement the efforts of all those who love and care for children." —*Childhood Education*

"Humorous and touching.... Excite[s] and educate[s]." —*Journal of the American Academy of Child and Adolescent Psychiatry*

"Children's hurts and concerns come alive.... Shows the power of play therapy and the importance of relationships." —*Psychology in the Schools*

"Bravo.... Speaks without jargon to both the layman and professional." —*The Arts in Psychotherapy*

"Vivid and captivating." —*Journal of Pediatric Psychology*

Teens in Therapy: Making It Their Own (W.W. Norton)

"A pleasure to read.... A suspenseful, engaging, and truly wise text." —Harry G. Segal, Ph. D., Cornell University

"Clearly written, down to Earth and at times humorous.... Bursting with real life examples of characters who howl, swear, make up fantastic stories and fall asleep through their sessions—but whom Bromfield portrays with respect and usually affection." —*Counselling Resource*

Doing Child and Adolescent Psychotherapy (Wiley)

"Extraordinary." —*Community Mental Health Journal*

"Humane, illustrative, and yet practical.... A pleasure to read." —*Child & Adolescent Social Work Journal*

"Enlightening and readable.... Engaging, fun, educational, and thought provoking." —*Journal of the American Academy of Child and Adolescent Psychiatry*

"Magnificent ... extremely well-written, insightful, engaging and educational." —*Bulletin of the Menninger Clinic*

Doing Therapy with Children and Adolescents with Asperger Syndrome (Wiley)

"Psychotherapy based on the practices described in this book will change the destiny of children and adults with Asperger's syndrome to one of greater connectivity to themselves and others. Should become the primary text for psychotherapists." —Tony Attwood, author of *The Complete Guide to Asperger's Syndrome*

"While explicitly informed by research, the strength of this book is the sense he gives the reader of participating, of being right inside these challenging yet tremendously productive therapy relationships along with himself and his young clients... The heart of therapy–keeping empathic however hard it might be–is beautifully expressed in this book. —*Counselling and Therapy Book Reviews*

How to Unspoil Your Child Fast (Sourcebooks)

"Offers practical advice with great empathy and wit, and shows parents how they can drastically improve their family life." —Rochelle Sharpe, Pulitzer Prize-winning journalist

"It's a lively, engaging, helpful book that offers a look at our generation of parents and why we're tempted to indulge our children." —*Cookie*

"It's a snappy read, so you can't claim you don't have time. And the method's simple, so you can't pretend you aren't qualified to use it." —*Newsday*

"It's a terrific book: logical, concrete, and easy to read." —*Boston Globe*

Embracing Asperger's: A Primer for Teachers and Professionals (Jessica Kingsley Publishers)

Coming in 2011...

HOW TO CITE
APA [*Style*]*6th*

IN PSYCHOLOGY,
SOCIAL WORK,
EDUCATION,
AND THE
SOCIAL SCIENCES

Richard Bromfield, Ph.D.
Harvard Medical School

Basil Books ❦ Boston

Library of Congress Cataloging-in-Publication Data
ISBN: 978-0-6155-4436-6
Bromfield, Richard.
How to cite APA [style]-6th in psychology, social work, education, and the social sciences / by Richard Bromfield.
1. Psychology–Authorship–Style manuals. 2. Social sciences–Authorship–Style manuals.
I. Title.

Design and typesetting: Arisman Design Studio

Printed in the United States by Basil Books, 47 Wolcott Road, Chestnut Hill, MA 02467.
http://www.basilbooks.com

Contents

Why I Wrote This Book   1
How to Use It   3
Good Writing, From Your Professor's Viewpoint   5
Why Is Writing Hard?   7

Alert! A Life-Saving (and Brief) Tour of Citation and References

Making Plagiarism Unnecessary   11
When You Don't Need to Cite   17
Cite Right, Cite Your Way   19
Handy Phrases for Citing   25
Block Quotes   29
How to Punctuate Citations   33
Citing Secondary Sources   35
Citing by Number of Authors, Etc.   37

General Reference Rules

Article and Book Titles   45
Order of References   47
Abbreviations   51
About the Publisher   53

References

Printed Sources   57
Online Sources   69
A Quick Side Trip on Editing   77
Formatting Your Paper   83
A Note on DOIs   85
References (Sample)   87
About the Author   89
Quick Chart for Citing and References   91
Quick Index to Citing and Reference   92

Why I Wrote This Book

Students and trainees would be happy to write and cite well, if only they knew how. Writing in the social sciences, especially the citing and reference part, can be a confusing, frustrating, and mind-numbing ordeal.

I have written this book to make perfectly clear, once and for all, how APA citation works. I want you to understand and see it as it is. Instead of being an exotic mystery for you to solve paper after paper, I want it to *make sense to you*, so you can do it easily and accurately. As an added bonus, you will then know what to note while doing your research,

saving you from that horrid task of retracing steps
to re-find your sources.

How to Use It

While putting hard work into your studies is admirable and worthwhile, the less suffering you experience while doing so, the better. This book aims and is set up to make your writing as painless as possible.

Students who just wish to get a paper done and out of the way can use this book as a rough-and-ready source to find an answer fast and easy. The quick index at the end of the book will take you to exactly the place in the book to find a clear illustration of how to cite and make reference to a specific type of source, and the quick guide on the next-to-last page will handle a majority of your citing and referencing needs.

Those who seek more, who strive for excellence, however, can use this book more as a primer and companion. By enlightening you as to the process and essence of APA style (6th ed.) and creative ways to use it, this guide will improve your writing and citing and make them second nature. You will come to own your growing competency, a skill that will make all of your writing clearer and easier, whatever the subject or project.

Either way, I suggest that you begin by scanning or browsing the book to see what it contains and how it's laid out. You'll decide for yourself which parts of the book can be of most use to you. You may find that some sections do the trick after one reading, whereas others are worth revisiting. Realizing that you have other work and a life too, I strove to write sections that are to the point, that go in easily and down fast. You may find it handy to insert sticky notes or flags in sections that especially suit your writing needs.

Last, if you go far in your studies, you will inevitably encounter citation and reference dilemmas not addressed in this guide. You will best consult the *Publication Manual of the American Psychological Association (6th ed.)*.

Good Writing, From Your Professor's Viewpoint

There is something you should know about your professors. Their passion is their subject matter, not teaching students how to write. However much students hate their professors marking their papers up in red and downgrading for weak writing or citing, their professors hate it even more. Professors have plenty to do without being the grammar or plagiarism police. In a perfect world imagined by professors, all students would come to their classes knowing how to write and cite properly. When reading your writing, it is what you have learned and what you have to say that interests them. Unfortunately, in a real world, professors cannot help but collide with, trip on, and suffer writing and citing that distracts from and undermines what a student like you tries to convey.

Why Is Writing Hard?

We all know how bad writer's block can be, staring at a blank page or screen, nothing happening. There are good reasons why you avoid your writing, and they often include feeling overwhelmed by a task and material that can loom enormous or vague.

Imagine building a home without tools or carpentry skills. You can't. Feeling overwhelmed, unequipped, and unskilled is enough to deter anyone. Growing competent and developing the skills to write and cite, however, can be a powerful antidote, not just to mediocre grades, but to feeling impotent and helpless.

By committing to learn the essentials of APA style, you'll grow into a more able, willing writer (and "citer").

ALERT!
A LIFE-SAVING (AND BRIEF) TOUR OF CITATION AND REFERENCE

By *life-saving*, I mean that taking this short tour can save you from future frustration, wasted time, downgrading, and the dire consequences of plagiarism. In short, *it's worth your time!*

Making Plagiarism Unnecessary

Simply put, plagiarism is presenting other people's words or ideas as if your own. In my experience, a majority of students plagiarize unintentionally, meaning they're not clear on what to cite and how to do it. But, whatever a student's reasons for plagiarizing, it represents a serious transgression that can lead to course failure, school expulsion, and—for those who care and I hope you do—a massive and likely irreparable loss of trust from your professor and faculty. By learning what and how to cite, you can eliminate the risk and temptation of plagiarism for your college career and the rest of your life.

11

Study the following brief examples until they fully make sense to you. If you can do that, the murky cloud over plagiarism will rise, and you will clearly see what you need to do to prevent it—*and why*.

We begin with *citation*. *Citing* means the way you present and denote the ideas or quotes in the actual text of your paper.

Study this example from Virginia Axline's 1947 classic *Play Therapy*:

> **Play therapy is based upon the fact that play is the child's natural medium of self-expression. It is an opportunity which is given to the child to "play out" his feelings and problems just as, in certain types of adult therapy, an individual "talks" out his difficulties. (1947, p. 9)**

*If from 1988 and pages 9-10,
I'd cite (1988, pp. 9-10).*

Consider these *acceptable* ways to use and cite what Axline wrote:

Children can use play to work out their feelings and problems (Axline, 1947).*

I don't need quotes, because I do not use Axline's exact words. I paraphrase her ideas in my own words.

---

*APA style recommends citing the page or, if none, the paragraph number even when paraphrasing. For now, most professors do not expect that. Follow your professor's guidelines.

Some compare children's play in therapy to adults' talking in therapy (Axline, 1947).

Likewise, I am not using an exact quote, but I borrow Axline's idea. I do not need quotes, but I still need to give her idea full credit.

If, as in the following examples, you use exact phrases or sentences, you need to use quotation marks and refer to the precise page number where the words come from.

According to Axline, "play therapy is based upon the fact that play is the child's natural medium of self-expression" (Axline, 1947, p. 9).

Axline saw children's playing in therapy to be "an opportunity which is given to the child to 'play out' his feelings and problems" (1947, p. 9).

I paraphrase—or reword—part of Axline's sentence but include an exact phrase in her words. I need quotation marks and page number. I change Axline's "play out" to 'play out' because that phrase falls between the double quotation marks used for the whole quote.

At least one clinician saw play as "the child's natural medium" to express herself (Axline, 1947, p. 9).

The variations in citation allow you to write flexibly and fluidly. For example, you may combine paraphrases and direct quotes in infinitely assorted ways.

Children's love of play can even find a useful place in the therapy room, where that natural way of expressing themselves can enable their "play[ing] out ... feelings and problems" (Axline, 1947, p. 9).

Notice all that I do, using brackets and ellipses, to incorporate both Axline's ideas and her exact words into a sentence that fits my tone, need, and style.

Brackets and ellipses enable you to edit and customize what you write to read well, while maintaining the integrity of the citation. You use [brackets] to add words to the original quote or to adapt it grammatically to suit your writing. You use ellipses (...) to signal that a word or words from the original quote are missing, that you've left something out purposely and knowingly. You do not need a bracket to change the case of the beginning letter of a quote or the punctuation at its end.

Using brackets and ellipses, you can write sentences like these:

Axline believed that "play therapy ... [exploits] ... the child's natural medium of self-expression" (1947, p. 9).

Axline believed that "play[ing in] therapy" takes advantage of "the child's natural medium of self-expression" (1947, p. 9).

Virginia Axline recognized "play therapy" as a form of treatment that, based on "the child's natural ... self-expression," can help her "to 'play out' [her] feelings and problems" (1947, p. 9).

> *Again, note that I use single quotation marks (' ') to quote material within double quotation marks.*

In 1947, Virginia Axline extolled the virtue of play in therapy for children. "Play," she wrote, "is the child's natural medium of self-expression" (p. 9). She went on to say that by doing so, "the child [can] 'play out' his feelings and problems" in the way that adults do so by talking (p. 9).

> *Note how I rework Axline's original paragraph, words, and ideas. With a responsible combination of exact quoting, paraphrasing, and brackets, I convey what Axline wrote in a different form that suits my*
> *(cont'd)*

style and makes for good readability. Because what I
write derives from a continuous discussion of Axline,
I need to cite the date only once in my paragraph. But
I cite the page number for each distinct quote

I hope that these examples begin to convince
you of the essential truth and simplicity of aca-
demic citation. As you can see, the possibilities are
endless. You can write easily and well, while citing
honestly and clearly.

All that matters is that I do
my utmost to honor—meaning to show—the
relationship of what I write to the original.

When You Don't
Need to Cite

You do not need to cite common knowledge, as in examples like these:

Boston, the capital of Massachusetts, is a great place to visit.

> *I can find a source, like an encyclopedia,
> that states the fact that Boston is the state
> capital of Massachusetts. But most of us know
> that fact, so I do not need to cite a source to justify
> my writing it. Nor do I need to cite a source
> for Boston being "a great place to visit."
> That is my opinion and idea.*

Likewise, and thinking back to the Axline excerpt on play therapy, you can safely write the following:

Children like to play.

Therapy can be helpful.

Children tend to play more, whereas adults talk more.

> *Though what I write touches upon Axline's ideas, mine are more general and pretty much common knowledge. However, it will never hurt me—or you—to overly cite or give credit to an original source. I cannot go wrong or be punished for crediting others.*

> *Be aware, however, you can also get into trouble for citing a source where the information or quote really doesn't come from. Sloppy or made-up citations are unacceptable.*

Cite Right,
Cite Your Way

Citing sources in your paper, essay, thesis, or whatever, can seem confusing and arbitrary—and rigid. It actually is not. It is flexible, and you can cite material in all kinds of ways to match your writing and style as well as to satisfy the APA 6th ed. guidelines for ethical and responsible writing.

To make this point perfectly clear in all of its possibilities, let's revisit the first sentence from Axline's excerpt on play therapy.

"Play therapy is based upon the fact that play is the child's natural medium of self-expression" **(Axline, 1947, p. 9).**

Examine this wide sampling of ethical ways to cite Axline's idea and words. They may seem repetitive, but each is unique. Spend a little time surveying and comparing these examples from what is a nearly endless world of possibility for using and citing Axline's one sentence. They all satisfy APA style. If you can grasp this variability and see why they are all acceptable, you are fast on your way to becoming a free, easy, and responsible "citer" of research and literature.

In 1947, Axline observed that "play is the child's natural medium of self-expression" (p. 9).

It is astonishing that more than a half a century ago, Virginia Axline wrote that "play is the child's natural medium of self-expression" (1947, p. 9).

Axline's recognition that children play to express themselves gave insight and purpose to the development of play therapy as a treatment modality (1947).

According to the child psychologist, Virginia Axline, play therapy exploits children's innate capacity to express themselves through their play (1947).

A child's playing is a capacity that we are told is natural and innate (Axline, 1947).

Play is how children express themselves (Axline, 1947).

While children also talk in therapy, their play, being the "natural medium [for their] self-expression," is central (Axline, 1947, p. 9).

Play therapy incorporates "play [as] the child's natural medium of self-expression" (Axline, 1947, p. 9).

If play is the "child's natural medium of self-expression" (Axline, 1947, p. 9), it makes us concerned for the child who lacks that seemingly human capacity, who appears unable to play.

I cite Axline midway through the
sentence, for she wrote about the first
part, but it was I, not she, who
posed the later question.

Axline (1947) wrote an entire book predicated on her basic belief that play can help children to express themselves in ways that bring insight, relief, and benefit.

"Play therapy," wrote Axline in 1947, "is based upon the fact that play is the child's natural medium of self-expression" (p. 9).

Axline said that "play is the child's natural medium of self-expression" (1947, p. 9).

Axline (1947) held that children use play to reveal who they are.

At least one prominent clinician told us that "play is the child's natural medium of self-expression" (Axline, 1947, p. 9).

Virginia Axline realized what an important self-representing function play serves for children (1947).

Play, Axline understood back in 1947, is how children express themselves and what they feel.

In 1947, Virginia Axline formally observed that play is the child's way to express herself.

Children need to play and need to express themselves (Axline, 1947).

Child therapists use play as a mode of treatment to help children express themselves (Axline, 1947).

If children's play is a "medium of [their] self-expression" (Axline, 1947, p. 9), what does that mean for the play of college students and adults?

When citing, do your best to cite ideas to the original source. Strive for accuracy. The point of citation is to give proper credit and to enable readers to find your sources, if they wish.

Keep in mind that APA style recommends citing the page or, if none, the paragraph number even when paraphrasing. For now, most professors do not expect that. Follow your professor's guidelines.

Handy Phrases
for Citing

To begin a sentence:

According to Axline
Axline says/said that
Axline believes/believed
Axline holds/held that
Axline purports/purported
Research suggests/suggested that
The literature shows/showed us that
Axline theorizes/theorized that
Axline hypothesizes/hypothesized that
Axline argues/argued that
Axline puts forth/put forth the notion
Axline conceptualizes/conceptualized

Axline surmises/surmised that
Axline takes/took as true that
Axline's work reveals/revealed
Observing [children] taught Axline that
Children showed Axline that
Axline articulates/articulated a view
Axline's view [of children] is/was that
Axline assumes/assumed that

Mid-sentence:

..., so understands/understood Axline,...
..., so goes/went Axline's thinking,...
..., writes/wrote Axline,...
..., Axline informs/informed us,...
..., Axline concludes/concluded,...
..., Axline goes/went on to say,...
..., continues/continued Axline,...

The tense of the verb—*concluded* or *concludes*, for instance—depends on the tone of your sentence and paragraph, and when the idea or sentence was originally written.

Variety is the spice of life and good writing. As you write your papers, experiment with different ways to cite properly. Cite in the beginning of a sentence, midway, and at the end. Try saying it differently, using different verbs, as I've illustrated above. Rather than simply list block quotes that can grow tedious for readers, strive to integrate cited ideas and writing with your own.

You can also vary how you refer to the date of origin. You can do it in parentheses, and usually that will do.

Axline (1947) believed play is a child's means of self-revelation.

However, you can do it in the text itself.

In 1947, Axline wrote about play and self-expression in children.

You can refer to time to help present a coherent history or give a perspective, as in the following examples, though you still must cite a year, precisely.

More than a half century ago, Axline (1947) sensed the importance of play to children and their self-expression.

Axline (1947) wrote about children, play, and self-expression decades before I myself had ever plowed my own hands through a sandbox.

Although toys have been around for centuries, it was not until fairly recently that the psychological functions of child's play were explored (Axline, 1947).

Once more I remind you: You can write with creativity and flexibility as long as you don't neglect to give proper credit, including quotation marks and page numbers when citing sentences or even parts of sentences exactly as you found them in the original source.

And if your professor prefers, follow APA style recommendation to cite the page or, if none, the paragraph number even when paraphrasing.

Block Quotes

You use a block quote when the material you are quoting is 40 words or more. With less than 40 words, you cite in the ways I've been describing and showing.

When citing a block quote:

(a) set the left margin inward 5 spaces for the entire block quote;
(b) do not indent the first line further, that is, you begin it flush at the indented left margin;
(c) double space the quote; and
(d) do not put quotation marks around the block quote.

This is how you cite Axline's excerpt in its entirety as a block quote:

Play therapy is based upon the fact that play is the child's natural medium of self-expression. It is an opportunity which is given to the child to "play out" his feelings and problems just as, in certain types of adult therapy, an individual "talks" out his difficulties. (Axline, 1947, p. 9)

> *Since I am not putting double quotation marks around the whole block quote, I am free to use the same double quotation marks around the phrases "play out" and "talks" that Axline used in her original writing.*

If the block quote has more than one paragraph, however, the first line of the second, third, and subsequent paragraphs are indented another 5 spaces, like this:

How else do I keep a child from spilling more than she wishes? When I am asked if I can keep a secret, or whether I want to hear one, I do not jump to answer, "Yes, yes." I curb my curiosity about the secret, but indulge my curiosity about the child's question:

"You wonder whether I can keep a secret?"

"You want to be careful about whom you tell secrets to?"

"What are you worried might happen after you tell me?" (Bromfield, 2010, p. 42)

> *After the un-indented first paragraph,*
> *I indent the first line of each succeeding*
> *paragraph an additional 5 spaces. Since I do*
> *not use double quotation marks around*
> *the block quote as a whole, I can use*
> *them around the dialogue, as the*
> *author did in the original.*

How to Punctuate Citations

By now you've seen dozens of ways to cite. Here is a short list to explicitly show how to punctuate citations:

Learning leads to improved behavior (Anderson, 2004).

I place the sentence-ending period after the (date).

In 2004, Anderson wrote about the benefits of learning.

Even simpler.

Anderson tells us that "learning is the path to
self-actualization" (2004, p. 34).

> *I put quote marks around the cited words,*
> *and place sentence-ending periods*
> *after the (date and page number).*

"Learning," wrote Anderson, "is the path to self-
actualization" (2004, p. 43).

> *I use multiple sets of quotes around*
> *interrupted cited material, still putting*
> *a period after the (date and page number).*

Some say that "learning is the path to self-actualization" (Anderson, 2004, p. 34), but I, like Miller,
believe it "is a product of mindful meditation"
(1996, p. 134).

> *This sentence, citing 2 different authors, is*
> *complicated. But I apply the same logic. I place*
> *quotes around the exact material, followed by*
> *parenthetically citing date and*
> *page number.*

Citing Secondary Sources

APA style strongly suggests that you search out and cite the original source of your quotation. When, however, you cannot find it, cite a secondary source as follows:

"The corridors and halls of almost any mainstream school are a constant tumult of noises echoing," so wrote Claire Sainsbury (2000, p. 101, as cited in Attwood, 2007, p. 272).

I give the original author, Claire Sainsbury,
full credit while also giving credit to Attwood,
specifically with date and page number,
for that is where I found her words.

If you choose to paraphrase or condense Sainsbury's idea, you can do this:

A school can be a sensorily noxious environment
for the child (Sainsbury, 2000, as cited in Attwood,
2007, p. 272).

> *Since I am not quoting exactly I do not*
> *need quotes or page number for Sainsbury,*
> *but I still need to show the exact*
> *source (date and page number) for*
> *Attwood, my original source.*

Citing by Number
of Authors, Etc.

1 author:

As Frith (1991) cautions, "Just how high is the cost, and how much effort is being spent in keeping up appearances?" (p. 22).

Teens with Asperger's can put in great effort at a high price to maintain a persona (Frith, 1991).

Frith (1991) wrote about teens, Asperger's, and image.

2 authors:

Parker and Asher (1993) emphasize the power
and positive influence to a child of one best friend.

> *When citing in text, I use "and"*
> *between the two authors' names.*

One best friend, in contrast to wide popularity,
can offer a child greater psychological benefit (Parker
& Asher, 1993).

> *I use an ampersand "&" when citing*
> *two authors within parentheses.*

3, 4, and 5 authors:

Carrington, Templeton, and Papincazak (2003)
examined the social implications of pretending to
be someone you are not, as applies to children with
Asperger syndrome.

Imagine a similar sentence with 4 or 5 names.
The names themselves can start to distract from
the clarity and meaning of the sentence itself. It be-
comes awkward reading.

When citing 3-5 authors, it is usually preferable
to go with parentheses.

First time cited within your paper:

"Masquerading" can be a stressful pursuit for adolescents with Asperger syndrome (Carrington, Templeton, & Papincazak, 2003, p. 216).

Again, I use an ampersand "&" within parentheses.

The second time you cite the same work, and beyond, you cite more simply:

(Carrington et al., 2003).

6 or more authors:

Leyfer et al. (2006) documented the strong association between Asperger's and anxiety symptoms in children.

Anxiety is commonly found in children with Asperger's (Leyfer et al., 2006).

It's my choice whether I incorporate the authors' names into the text proper or at the end within parentheses.

Organization or group as author:

Books are commonly "authored" by professional groups, universities, and so forth. Here are examples for citing such a work:

In 1994, Asperger's Disorder was made an official diagnosis in the DSM-IV (American Psychiatric Association, [APA], 1994).

> *If you cite the same text again, abbreviate: (APA, 1994). See page 65* [**R16**] *for more.*

The *Merriam-Webster's Collegiate Dictionary* (1998) defines safety as "the condition of being safe from undergoing or causing hurt, injury, or loss" (p. 1027).

The penalties for plagiarism in this community are clearly spelled out (University of Northwestern Massachusetts, 2005).

More than one author cited at once:

Research proves what we all have long known, that children are driven by curiosity and a love of learning (Hassan, Bates, Bankley, Medford, & Hotchkins, 2007; Haspers, 2010).

More than one work by one author:

A sequence of innovative studies shows us that children are truly curious creatures (Simpson 1998, 1999a, 1999b).

> *I specify the original works in my References as 1999a and 1999b to distinguish more than one work published in the same year by the same author.*

Personal communication:

You may wish to include ideas or quotes that you receive in a letter, email, as comments on a paper or manuscript, or in a discussion with another person. You must give credit to that source and individual.

As Professor M. Georgeworth warned me, "psychology can be put to good use and to bad use" (personal communication, April 11, 2009).

"It's easy to forget to give proper credit, and to actually come to believe that some idea that you borrowed is your own" (R. N. Bromfield, personal communication, December 18, 2010).

> *I don't specify the type of personal communication. I give credit only by name and date. I do not include personal communications in the References.*

The Bible:

You cite Bible text by book, chapter, verses, line, and canto. The first time in a paper—and only the first time—you specify which version of the Bible you use.

"But now abideth," the Bible says, "faith, hope, love these three; and the greatest of these is love" (I Cor. 13:13, American Standard Version).

> *For subsequent quotes from that version of the Bible, I cite only the location.*

The Bible reads, "Follow after love; yet desire earnestly spiritual gifts, but rather that ye may prophesy" (I Cor. 14:1).

Reprint (earlier original):

If a book was first printed in 1944, but you use a reprint from 1991, you cite as:

The disorder was first chronicled by a Viennese pediatrician (Asperger, 1944/1991).

GENERAL
REFERENCES RULES

Article and Book Titles

Journal article with no subtitle:

Gillberg, C. (1989). Asperger syndrome in 23 Swedish children. *Developmental Medicine and Child Neurology, 31*(4), 520-531. doi:10.1111/j.1469-8749.1989.tb04031.x

> *Capitalize the first letter of an article title and any words in title that are usually capitalized (e.g. Swedish).*

> *Capitalize and italicize every word in the journal title, except "and."*

> *Italicize volume number.*

> *Do not italicize page number and do not write p. or pp.*

Journal article with subtitle:

Henley, D. (2000). Blessings in disguise: Idiomatic expression as a stimulus in group art therapy with children. *Art Therapy, 17*(4), 270-275.

> *Capitalize the first letter of both article title and subtitle.*
>
> *See pages 85-86 for rules when a DOI is unavailable.*

Book titles:

Sainsbury, C. (2000). *Martian in the playground: Understanding the schoolchild with Asperger's syndrome.* Bristol, England: Lucky Duck Publishing.

> *Capitalize the first letter of both book title and subtitle.*
>
> *Italicize both book title and subtitle.*
>
> *Capitalize words in the title that are usually capitalized, such as the terms "Asperger," "Rome," and "George Washington."*

Order of References

References are alphabetized by author name:

Attwood, T. (2000). Strategies for...
Bromfield, R. (2007). *Playing for...*
Piaget, J. (1954). *The construction...*

For one author with more than one publication, start with the earliest date:

Attwood, T. (2000). Strategies for...
Attwood, T. (2003). Frameworks for...
Attwood, T. (2007). *The complete guide...*

For one author, with co-authors too, successively alphabetize by second co-author's name, then third, and so forth:

Bauminger, N. (2004). The expression...
Bauminger, N., Chomsky-Smolkin, L., Orbach-Caspi, E., Zachor, D., & Levy-Shiff, R. (2008). Jealousy and emotional...
Bauminger, N., & Kasari, C. (2000). Loneliness and...
Bauminger, N., Shulman, C., & Agam, G. (2003). Peer interaction and loneliness...
Bauminger, N., Solomon, M., Aviezer, A., Heung, K., Brown, J., & Rogers, S. (2008). Friendship in high-functioning...

If two articles are identically co-authored, start with earliest date:

Francesco, I., & Russo, P. (1998). Differences in imagery...
Francesco, I., & Russo, P. (2001). Imagery as associated...

For works by authors with the same last name, alphabetize by first initial:

Majic, S. (2005). *Economic indicators*...
Majic, W. (2001). Longterm studies of...

For one author's works published in the same year, use a, b, c, and so on:

Attwood, T. (2004a). *Exploring feelings: Cognitive behavior therapy to manage anger...*
Attwood, T. (2004b). *Exploring feelings: Cognitive behavior therapy to manage anxiety...*

For works written by an association or group, alphabetize with first word of group's name:

Allen, F. H. (1964). The beginning phase...
American Psychiatric Association. (1994) *Diagnostic and statistical manual...*
Axline, V. (1969). *Play therapy...*

> *Note that "American" alphabetically comes between "Allen" and "Axline."*

For the purposes of space, the example references in this book have been single-spaced. According to APA style, your references should be *double-spaced* and formatted with a *hanging indent.* (See sample References on pages 87-88.)

Abbreviations

Editor	Ed.
Editors	Eds.
Revised edition	Rev. ed.
Second edition	2nd ed.
Translator(s)	Trans.
No date	n.d.
Page	p.
Pages	pp.
Volume	Vol.
Number	No.
Supplement	Suppl.

About the Publisher

For books published in the United States and Canada, you identify both the city and the state or province:

Gladwell, M. (2005). *Blink.* New York, NY: Back Bay Books.

Madigan, S. (2010). *Narrative therapy.* Washington, DC: American Psychological Association.

Epstein, M. (2007). *Psychotherapy without the self: A Buddhist perspective.* New Haven, CT: Yale University Press.

Brown, I. (2009). *The boy in the moon.* Toronto, ON: Random House Canada.

For publishers in countries other than the US that also have states, you need to mention the city, state, and country:

Trotter, C. (2004). *Helping abused children and their families.* Sydney, NSW, Australia: Allen & Unwin.

For publishers in countries other than the US, Canada, and those with states:

Shailor, J. (2010). *Performing new lives: Prison theatre.* London, England: Jessica Kingsley.

When publisher is a state university press, you need only mention the city of publication:

Bernstein, J. (2010). *Rachel in the world.* Champaign: University of Illinois Press.

When documenting the publisher's name, leave out unnecessary words, including: Publishers, Company, Incorporated, Sons (or abbreviations of these). Retain words such as Press and Books.

REFERENCES

Printed Sources*

Journal article, 1 author   [R1]

In References:

Frith, U. (2001). Mind blindness and the brain in
   autism. *Neuron, 32,* 969-979. doi:10.1016/
   S0896-6273(01)00552-9

In Text:

Frith (2001) believes that...

paraphrase (Frith, 2001).

"exact quote" (Frith, 2001, p. 23).

*See pages 85-86 to learn rules of DOIs. *Remember:* APA style does
not require but recommends citing page or paragraph number even
for paraphrasing. Follow your professor's guidelines.

[R2]   **Journal article, 2 authors**

In References:

Thede, L., & Coolidge, F. (2007). Psychological and neurobehavioral comparisons of children with Asperger's disorder versus high-functioning autism. *Journal of Autism and Developmental Disorders, 37*(5), 847-854. doi:10.1007/s10803-006-0212-0

In Text:

Thede and Coolidge (2007) wrote that...

paraphrase (Thede & Coolidge, 2007).

"exact quote" (Thede & Coolidge, 2007, p. 848).

[R3]   **Journal article, 3 to 5 authors**

In References:

Towbin, K., Pradella, A., Gorrindo, T., Pine, D., & Liebenluft, E. (2005). Autistic spectrum traits in children with mood and anxiety disorders. *Journal of Child and Adolescent Psychopharmacology, 15*(3), 452-464. doi:10.1089/cap.2005.15.452

In Text, first time:

Towbin, Pradella, Gorrindo, Pine, and Liebenluft (2005) found that...

paraphrase (Towbin, Pradella, Gorrindo, Pine, & Liebenluft, 2005).

"exact quote" (Towbin, Pradella, Gorrindo, Pine, & Liebenluft, 2005, pp. 453-454).

In Text, second and successive times:

Towbin et al. (2005) studied...

paraphrase (Towbin et al., 2005).

"exact quote" (Towbin et al., 2005, p. 462).

Journal article, 6 or 7 authors   [R4]

In References:

Klin, A., Saulnier, C., Sparrow, S., Cicchetti, D., Volkmar, F., & Lord, C. (2007). Social and communication abilities and disabilities in higher functioning individuals with autism spectrum disorders: The Vineland and the ADOS. *Journal of Autism and Developmental Disorders, 37*(4), 748-759. doi:10.1007/s10803-006-0229-4

Include all 6 or 7 authors' names.

In Text:

Klin et al. (2007) found that...

paraphrase (Klin et al., 2007).

"exact quote" (Klin et al., 2007, p. 757).

[R5]   **Journal article, 8 or more authors**

In References:

Lord, C., Risi, S., Lambrecht, L., Cook, E.,
    Leventhal, B., DiLavore, P.,...Rutter, M.
    (2000). The Autism Diagnostic Observation
    Schedule—Generic: A standard measure of
    social and communication deficits associated
    with the spectrum of autism. *Journal of
    Autism and Developmental Disorders, 30*(3),
    205–223. doi:10.1023/A:1005592401947

> *List the first 6 names, followed by
> an ellipsis (3 periods, like...), then
> list the final author's name.*

In Text:

Lord et al. (2000) suggested that...

paraphrase (Lord et al., 2000).

"exact quote" (Lord et al., 2000, p. 211).

[R6]   **Magazine article**

In References:

Gardner, H. (1981, December). Do babies sing a
    universal song? *Psychology Today, 15*, 70-76.

In Text:

Gardner (1981) wrote a piece on...

paraphrase (Gardner, 1981).

"exact quote" (Gardner, 1981, p. 72).

Newspaper article with author   [R7]

In References:

Nichols, W. (2010, October 17). A new lens. *The Boston Globe*, p. K2.

In Text:

Nichols (2010) explained that...

paraphrase (Nichols, 2010).

"exact quote" (Nichols, 2010, p. K2).

If article has interrupted pages:

In References:

Cullen, K. (2010, October 17). Unleash the dogs of capitalism. *The Boston Globe*, pp. K1, K3.

In Text:

Cullen (2010) wrote that...

paraphrase (Cullen, 2010).

"exact quote" (Cullen, 2010, p. K3).

Newspaper article without author   [R8]

In References:

Saturdays in the hospital. (2010, October 17). *The Boston Globe*, p. K8.

(*cont'd*)

In Text:

Create a short title based on actual title.

paraphrase ("Saturdays in Hospital," 2010).

"exact quote"("Saturdays in Hospital," 2010, p. K8).

[R9]   **Abstract from original journal article**

In References:

Freed, C. R. (2010). Addiction medicine and
    addiction psychiatry in America [Abstract].
    Contemporary Drug Problems, 37, 25.

In Text:

Freed (2010) suggested that...

paraphrase (Freed, 2010).

"exact quote" (Freed, 2010, p. 25).

[R10]   **Book, 1 author**

In References:

Gardner, H. (2006). *Multiple intelligences: New
    horizons in theory and practice.* New York,
    NY: Basic.

In Text:

Gardner (2006) conceptualized...

paraphrase (Gardner, 2006).

"exact quote" (Gardner, 2006, p. 234).

Book, 2 authors   [R11]

In References:

Bashe, P., & Kirby, B. (2001). *The Oasis guide to
    Asperger syndrome.* New York, NY: Crown.

In Text:

Bashe and Kirby (2001) wrote that...

paraphrase (Bashe & Kirby, 2001).

"exact quote" (Bashe & Kirby, 2001, p. 56).

Book, 3-5 authors   [R12]

In References:

Myles, B., Cook, K., Miller, N., Rinner, L., &
    Robbins, L. (2000). *Asperger syndrome and
    sensory issues.* Shawnee Mission, KS: Autism
    Asperger Publishing.

In Text, first time:

Myles, Cook, Miller, Rinner, and Robbins (2000)
studied...

*But this is awkward.
It is better to use parentheses.*

paraphrase (Myles, Cook, Miller, Rinner, & Robbins,
2000).

"exact quote" (Myles, Cook, Miller, Rinner, &
Robbins, 2000, p. 122).

(cont'd)

In Text, second time and beyond:

Myles et al. (2000) developed...

paraphrase (Myles et al., 2000).

"exact quote" (Myles et al., 2000, pp. 110-111).

[R13]   **Book, 6 or 7 authors**

In References:

Bambers, H., Evans, J., Mino, T., Callaway, A., Rasputin, H., Klinko, F., & Dewsome, T. (2002). *Behavior modification from new perspectives.* Memphis, TN: Insight.

In Text:

Bambers et al. (2002) innovated a new...

paraphrase (Bambers et al., 2002).

"exact quote' (Bambers et al., 2002, p. 5).

[R14]   **Book, 8 or more authors**

In References:

Tam, F., Xu, L., Wood, W., Mix, R., Ede, T., Ollie, R.,...Smithers, Q. (2003). *Levity.* Portland, ME: All-Heal Press.

> *List the first 6 names, followed by an ellipsis (...) then the final author's name.*

In Text:

Tam et al. (2003) suggest that...

paraphrase (Tam et al., 2003).

"exact quote" (Tam et al., 2003, p. 177).

Book, no author [R15]

In References:

Merriam-Webster's Collegiate Dictionary (10th ed.). (1998). Springfield, MA: Merriam-Webster.

In Text:

Merriam-Webster (1998) defined...

"definition" (Merriam-Webster, 1998, p. 344).

Book, group or organization as author [R16]

In References:

American Psychological Association. (2010). *Publication manual of the American Psychological Association* (6ᵗʰ ed.). Washington, DC: Author.

In Text:

According to the American Psychological Association (2010),

paraphrase (American Psychological Association, 2010).

"exact quote" (American Psychological Association, 2010, pp. 30-31). *(cont'd)*

The first time, spell out the group author's name.
Subsequently, use acronym or abbreviation if easy
to recognize. For example: (APA, 2010).

[R17]   **Book, edited**

In References:

Baron-Cohen, S., Tager-Flusberg, H., & Cohen, D.
(Eds.) (2000). *Understanding other minds:*
Perspectives from autism and developmental
cognitive neuroscience. Oxford, England:
Oxford University Press.

In Text:

Baron-Cohen, Tager-Flusberg, and Cohen (2000)
wrote about…

paraphrase (Baron-Cohen, Tager-Flusberg, &
Cohen, 2000).

"exact quote" (Baron-Cohen, Tager-Flusberg, &
Cohen, 2000, p. 199).

[R18]   **Chapter, from edited book**

In References:

Kasari, C., Chamberlain, B., & Bauminger, N.
(2001). Social emotions and social
relationships in Autism: Can children with
Autism compensate? In J. Burack, T.
Charman, N. Yirmiya, & P. Zelazo (Eds.),

Development and Autism: Perspectives from theory and research (pp. 309-333). Mahwah, NJ: Erlbaum.

In Text:

Kasari, Chamberlain, and Bauminger (2001) view...

paraphrase (Kasari, Chamberlain, & Bauminger, 2001).

"exact quote" (Kasari, Chamberlain, & Bauminger, 2001, p. 322).

Book, translated into English   [R19]

In References:

Piaget, J. (1985). *The equilibration of cognitive structures* (T. Brown & K.J. Thampy, Trans.). Chicago, IL: University of Chicago Press. (Original work published 1975)

In Text:

paraphrase (Piaget, 1975/1985).

"exact quote" (Piaget, 1975/1985, p. 34).

Book, reprint   [R20]

In References:

Winnicott, D.W. (2005). *The maturational processes and the facilitating environment.* New York, NY: Routledge. (Original work published 1971)   *(cont'd)*

In Text:

paraphrase (Winnicott, 1971/2005).

"exact quote" (Winnicott, 1971/2005, p. 182).

[R21]   **Book review**

In References:

Moore, C. (2003, May 24). Just the facts, ma'am. [Review of the book *The curious incident of the dog in the night-time,* by M. Haddon]. *The Guardian,* 33.

In Text:

Moore (2003) wrote that...

paraphrase (Moore, 2003).

"exact quote" (Moore, 2003, p. 33).*

---

*For reviews of articles, videos, and videogames, see the *Publication Manual of the American Psychological Association* (6th ed.) (2010, pp. 208-209).

Online Sources[*]

Online article based on printed journal [R22]

Technically speaking, and though usually identical to the original in the printed journal, a journal article you find online should be identified as such.

In References:

Lyons, V., & Fitzgerald, M. (2007). Asperger (1906-1980) and Kanner (1894-1981), the two pioneers of autism. *Journal of Autism and Developmental Disorders, 37*(10), 2022-2023. doi:10.1007/s10803-007-0383-3

(*cont'd*)

In Text:

Lyons and Fitzgerald (2007) wrote that...

paraphrase (Lyons & Fitzgerald, 2007).

"exact quote" (Lyons & Fitzgerald, 2007, p. 2022).

[R23]   **Online article from internet-only journal**

In References:

Young, T.M. (2008, July). The big-seven early
    markers for childhood-onset psychosis
    spectrum disorders. *Child Psychiatry Online.*
    Retrieved from http://www.priory.com/
    psychiatry/childhood_onset_psychosis.htm

In Text:

Young (2008) wrote about...

paraphrase (Young, 2008).

"exact quote" (Young, 2008, para #).

There is no page number to cite.

[R24]   **Online informational website with author**

In References:

Boyse, K. (2009, November). Non-verbal learning
    disability (NLD or NVLD). *Your Child:
    Development & Behavior Resources.* Retrieved
    from http://www.med.umich.edu/yourchild/
    topics/nld.htm

In Text:

Boyse (2009) discussed...

paraphrase (Boyse, 2009).

"exact quote" (Boyse, 2009, para. #).

No page number to cite.

Online informational website, no author   [R25]

In References:

Epilepsy and the brain. (n.d.). Epilepsy.com.
    Retrieved from http://www.epilepsy.com/
    epilepsy/epilepsy_brain

Use n.d. to represent no date available.

In Text:

paraphrase ("Epilepsy and the Brain," n.d.).

"exact quote" ("Epilepsy and the Brain," n.d.,
para #).

Article, from online magazine   [R26]

In References:

Underwood, A. (2008, July 8). Prozac nation no
    more? *Newsweek.* Retrieved from http://
    www.newsweek.com/

*Use simple and short URL when
article can be readily found there.*

(cont'd)

> *If there was a month but no day,*
> *cite like (2008, July).*

In Text:

Underwood (2008) wrote...

paraphrase (Underwood, 2008).

"exact quote" (Underwood, 2008, para. #).

> *No page number to cite.*

[R27]   **Article, from online newspaper**

In References:

Belluck, P. (2010, November 1). For youth,
    depression often has a sequel. *New York
    Times.* Retrieved from http://www.nytimes.
    com

> *Use simple and short URL when*
> *article can be readily found there.*

In Text:

Belluck wrote in 2010 that...

paraphrase (Belluck, 2010).

"exact quote" (Belluck, 2010, para. #).

> *No page number to cite.*

Dissertations & Theses [R28]

In References:

Tucker, J. (2009). The correlation between Myers-
Briggs type and preparedness for leadership
(Doctoral dissertation). Retrieved from
ProQuest Dissertations & Theses database.
(AAT 3362656)

> *Or, (Master's thesis), followed by the name
> of the database, and the accession, order,
> or publication number.*

In Text:

Tucker (2009) studied...

paraphrase (Tucker, 2009).

"exact quote" (Tucker, 2009, pp. 45-46).

Encyclopedia [R29]

In References:

Plagiarism. (2010). In *Encyclopedia Britannica.*
Retrieved from http://www.britannica.com/
EBchecked/topic/462640/plagiarism

> *Wikipedia as a source is frowned upon.*

In Text:

paraphrase ("Plagiarism," 2010).

"exact quote" ("Plagiarism," 2010, para. 1).

[R30]   **Online lecture or speech**

In References:

Rowling, J. K. (2008, June 5). The fringe benefits
of failure, and the importance of imagination.
Speech presented at Harvard University
graduation ceremony, Cambridge, MA.
[Transcript]. Retrieved from http://
harvardmagazine.com/commencement/
the-fringe-benefits-failure-the-importance-
imagination

In Text:

J. K. Rowling (2008) spoke about...

paraphrase (Rowling, 2008).

"exact quote" (Rowling, 2008, para. #).

No page number to cite.

[R31]   **Online TV or radio***

In References:

Flatow, I. (Host). (2010, July 9). Building new
neurons [Radio transcript]. Washington, DC:
National Public Radio. Retrieved from http://
www.sciencefriday.com/program/
archives/201007093

---

*To cite podcasts and other audiovisual media, see the *Publication
Manual of the American Psychological Association* (6th ed.) (2010, pp.
209-210).

In Text:

> Ira Flatow (2010) explained that...
>
> paraphrase (Flatow, 2010).
>
> "exact quote" (Flatow, 2010).

No page to cite.

Online posting or blog entry   [R32]

In References:

Belkin, L. (2010, October 28). Mother's brains are
bigger [Web log post]. Retrieved from http://
parenting.blogs.nytimes.com/

In Text:

> Lisa Belkin (2010) wrote...
>
> paraphrase (Belkin, 2010).
>
> "exact quote" (Belkin, 2010, para #).

No page number to cite.

If a web log comment:

Edwards, H. (2010, October 28). Re: Mother's
brains are bigger [Online forum comment].
Retrieved from http://parenting.blogs.
nytimes.com/

[R33]   **Personal communication**

In References:

You do not include personal communications in the References.

In Text:

As Professor M. Georgeworth warned me, "psychology can be put to good use and to bad use" (personal communication, April 11, 2009).

[R34]   **The Bible**

In References:

Do not include common religious texts—such as the Bible and the Qur'an—in the References.

In Text:

As I Corinthians 13:13 states, "But now abideth faith, hope, love these three; and the greatest of these is love" (American Standard Version).

Subsequent quotes from that version of the Bible require only that the passage source be cited. However, when a different version is used, that version must be identified.

A Quick Side Trip
on Editing

If you want a higher grade, a happier professor, or, dare I say, to be a stronger writer, there is only one way, and that is to edit and revise your writing, over and over. It is hard to face one's work and mistakes, because you then have to fix them. For good or bad, the reality is certain. If you want better for yourself and your writing, you are going to have to bite the bullet—*and edit.*

Warning:
I realize that few of you will pay much
attention to these rules, nor will you apply
them. That's too bad, for students who commit to
editing nearly always get better grades and get
better at writing.

Rule #1: Take your editing seriously

As long as you see editing as a pain in the rear or as writing's poorer cousin or as just something to get through quickly, you and your writing are doomed. The sooner you surrender to the process, the sooner your writing will soar.

Rule #2: Change your hat

To be both writer and critic is a conflict of interest. As writer, you want your critic to love what you've written. You want to hear praise. You don't want to hear advice or that you have more work to do. As critic, you want the space and freedom to be cool-headed and cold-blooded without having to worry about hurting the writer's feelings.

Try to forget you are the writer when editing your work. Edit your writing as if it's someone else's, someone else who'll have to fix it. Try to imagine you are a writing teacher or your professor. Hold your re-writing until after you've edited. Instead, just proofread, marking what's wrong or noting places that read confusing, disjointed, awkward, etc. You'll have time to respond to "your critic's" comments after you get your paper back from your own edit.

Rule #3: Change your seat

Do your editing in a different place than you do your writing. If you can, perhaps, change rooms or chairs. Try to take at least a small break after writing and before editing. Strive to find a position where you are comfortable yet alert, with enough light to read easily. You may prefer a stiff clipboard to hold your papers. When working at night, editing under a reading lamp can help you focus on the writing.

Rule #4: Use paper and double or triple spacing

Bother to print your word-processing out on paper. Avoid editing your writing on the screen. Print your draft using good-sized margins and triple spacing between lines. This will give you plenty of room to edit and make comments that you can later read.

Rule #5: Use a colored pencil

Buy a colored pencil that you like. It doesn't have to be red. Use it only to edit. You will train yourself to see that pencil as having special powers in your hands. Keep the point sharp. Take care to write legibly, for this can facilitate your thinking clearly.

Rule #6: Assume nothing

Don't take anything for granted. Proofread and edit everything, however tedious, even all those periods and 3-letter words that seem above questioning. You may think they are too commonplace or obvious to bother with, but they're not. You won't remember to fix them otherwise.

Rule #7: Look it up

Writing is nothing but stringing words together to say something intentional. The specific words you use matter. When you are unsure about a word or a phrase or some point of grammar, look it up. Whether you use a dictionary, the *Elements of Style*, Google, or www.dictionary.com makes no difference. By looking it up, you'll get it right today, get it right tomorrow, and gain confidence in your writing.

Rule #8: Read aloud

When you read silently to yourself, you can fool yourself without meaning to. You know what you want to say and so unconsciously fill in the blanks. You read "the" where it's missing or "they're" as "their." When you read aloud, you inevitably bump into your errors. You find yourself lost in sentences that make little sense or sound more like the dialogue of illiterate characters. You struggle to read words that, even if your own, you can neither pronounce nor decipher. You gasp for air where commas are needed or trip over repeated and misplaced commas like so many mischievous children's legs.

Reading aloud forces you, as writer, to face your writing and allows you to hear the rhythm and rhyme of what you've done.

Some writers prefer to read the last draft aloud, using that method to apply a final polish to their work.

Rule #9: Be consistent

Strive in all ways to edit in a consistent fashion. Use the same editing chair, pencil, light, table, etc. Use the same proofreading marks—the official ones or your own—to mark up your writing. Attack your writing in a systematic way that makes sense to you. Look for the same types of errors, big and small, every time you edit. By this repetitive training, your editing skills will become second-nature to your writing.

Rule #10: Keep track

Few things are as frustrating, discouraging, and maddening as losing a document or confusing earlier and later versions. Be organized and careful. Take the time to think up and type out file names that make sense and identify the writing project (e.g. <mazes&learning-draft#1- 3.04.11>). Set your word processor to make back-up copies and do frequent auto saves. Invest in a cheap flash stick or key card to back up your writing every time you work on it. For bigger or longer projects, consider labeling your paper with a running page header, the date of which you change each time you revise (e.g. "mazes&learning-may4"). Also, know that most current word processors can rescue writing you've done should the program or your computer crash. Many students prefer Google Docs to write their papers (http://docs.google.com/). Google Docs can be accessed from any computer and automatically keeps track of every version you work on.

Formatting Your Paper

Use Times New Roman (12 point) unless, of course, your professor or school suggests otherwise.

Leave margins of at least 1 inch (2.54 cm) on left, right, top, and bottom.

Double-space everywhere.

Leave 1 space after commas, semicolons, and colons anywhere in the paper. In references, leave 1 space after all periods. For papers: everywhere but in the references, leave 1 or 2 spaces after periods (unless your professor or school has a preference). For manuscripts submitted to journals: leave 2 spaces after periods ending sentences. Consult the writer's guidelines of any specific journal you submit to.

A simple 3-tier system of headings will satisfy most of your writing needs.

1. (Title) Center, boldface, mix of capital and lowercase.
2. Flush left, boldface, mix of capital and lowercase letters.
3. Indent, boldface, lowercase, end in period.
4. *If a 4th level of heading is needed:* indent, boldface, italicize, capitalize the first letter then use lowercase, and end in a period.

Headings might look like this:

Results

Gains in Cognition

Gifted and talented programs.
Teaching to the middle.

Gains in Emotional Development

Cognition and feeling.
Experiential learning.

As you have noticed, for reasons of design and appeal, I do not not employ the APA system of headings in this book. [*]

---

[*] Formatting guidelines from: American Psychological Association. (2010). *Publication manual of the American Psychological Association* (6th ed.). Washington, DC: Author.

A Note on DOIs

For the sake of ease, reliability, and consistency, sources are being assigned a Digital Object Identifier (DOI). This number assigns the source an address on the Internet. The DOI is more dependable than unwieldy URL addresses that can themselves change or go extinct.

When it is available, you may be able to find the DOI in the citation, abstract, or first page of an article or book. Even when your source is a printed journal, you are encouraged to seek the DOI. Once your paper is written, you can "search on article title" at www.crossref.org to find the DOI, if it exists for your source.

If there is a DOI (whether from print or online):

Benton, C. (2010). Rapid reactions to direct and
    averted facial expressions of fear and anger.
    Visual Cognition, 18(9), 1298-1319. doi:10.10
    80/13506285.2010.481874

No period at the end.

If there is no DOI and you found the source in print:

Kanner, L. (1943). Autistic disturbances of
    affective contact. *Nervous Child, 2,* 217-250.

If there is no DOI and you found the source online,
cite the journal's home page URL:

Notman, M.T. (2006). Mothers and daughters as
    adults. *Psychoanalytic Inquiry, 26*(1), 137-153.
    Retrieved from http://www.informaworld.
    com/smpptitle~content=t783567627~db=all

No retrieval date is needed.

If an online source has no page numbers, cite
quoted material by paragraph number, such as:
(Donovan, 2005, para. 3). See the *Publication Man-*
ual of the American Psychological Association (6th ed.)
(2010, pp. 171-172).

References (Sample)

Attwood, T. (2007). *The complete guide to Asperger's syndrome*. Philadelphia, PA: Jessica Kingsley.

Axline, V. (1969). *Play therapy*. New York, NY: Ballentine.

Baranek, G., Foster, L., & Berkson, G. (1997). Sensory defensiveness in persons with developmental disabilities. *Occupational Therapy Journal of Research, 17*(3), 173-185.

Baron-Cohen, S. (1987). Autism and symbolic play. *British Journal of Developmental Psychology, 5*(2), 139-148.

Baron-Cohen, S. (1989). The autistic child's theory of mind: A case of specific developmental delay. *Journal of Child Psychology and Psychiatry, 30*(2), 285-297. doi:10.1111/j.1469-7610.1989.tb00241.x

Baron-Cohen, S, (2007). I cannot tell a lie. *In Character, 3*, 52-59.

Bauminger, N. (2004). The expression and understanding of jealousy in children with Autism. *Development and Psychopathology, 16*(1), 157-177. doi:10.1017/S0954579404044451

Bauminger, N., & Kasari, C. (2000). Loneliness
    and friendship in high-functioning children
    with Autism. *Child Development, 71*(2),
    447-456. doi:10.1111/1467-8624.00156

Bauminger, N., Shulman, C., & Agam, G. (2003).
    Peer interaction and loneliness in high-
    functioning children with Autism. *Journal of
    Autism and Developmental Disorders, 33*(5),
    489-507. doi:10.1023/A:1025827427901

Bemporad, J., Ratey, J., & O'Driscoll, G. (1987).
    Autism and emotion: An ethological theory.
    American Journal of Orthopsychiatry, 57(4),
    477-483. doi:10.1111/j.1939-0025.1987.
    tb03563.x

Bleuler, E. (1950). *Dementia praecox or the group
    of Schizophrenias* (J. Zikin, Trans.). New York,
    NY: International Universities Press.
    (Original work published 1911)

Blomberg, B. (2005). Time, space, and the mind:
    Psychotherapy with children with Autism. In
    D. Houzel & M. Rhode (Eds.), *Invisible
    boundaries: Psychosis and Autism in children
    and adolescents* (pp. 25-42). London,
    England: Karnac.

*Remember! References use hanging
indent, double line-spacing, and 1 space after
punctuation (commas, colons, and periods).*

About the Author

Richard Bromfield, Ph.D., is a graduate of Bowdoin College and the University of North Carolina at Chapel Hill. A member of the faculty of Harvard Medical School, he writes about children, psychotherapy, family life, and Asperger syndrome for clinicians, parents, educators, and general readers.

Quick Chart for Citing and References

In-Text Citing

	1st use	2nd, 3rd,...
1 author	Tam (2003)	same
2	Tam and Xu (2003)	same
3-5	Tam, Xu, Wood, and Mix (2003)	Tam et al. (2003)
6+	Tam et al. (2003)	same

(In-Text Citing)

	1st time	2nd, 3rd,...
1	(Tam, 2003)	same
2	(Tam & Xu, 2003)	same
3-5	(Tam, Xu, Wood, & Mix, 2003)	(Tam et al., 2003)
6+	(Tam et al., 2003)	same

References

1	Tam, F. (2003). ...
2	Tam, F., & Xu, L. (2003). ...
3-7	Tam, F., Xu, L., Wood, W., & Mix, R. (2003). ...
8+	Tam, F., Xu, L., Wood, W., Mix, R., Ede, T., Ollie, R., ... Smithers, Q. (2003). ...

Quick Index to Citing
and References

Journals/Periodicals
1 author [R1]
2 authors [R2]
3-5 authors [R3]
6 or 7 authors [R4]
8 or more authors [R5]
Magazine article [R6]
Newspaper article
   with author [R7]
   without author [R8]
Abstract, journal [R9]

Books
1 author [R10]
2 authors [R11]
3-5 authors [R12]
6 or 7 authors [R13]
8 or more authors [R14]
no author [R15]
by organization/group [R16]
edited [R17]
chapter [R18]
translated to English [R19]
reprint [R20]
review [R21]

Online (Internet)
Article,
   print journal [R22]
   Internet-only [R23]
Informational website
   with author [R24]
   without author [R25]
Magazine article [R26]
Newspaper article [R27]
Dissertations & Theses [R28]
Encyclopedia [R29]
Lecture or speech [R30]
TV or radio [R31]
Posting or blog entry [R32]

Other
Pers. communications [R33]
The Bible [R34]

Made in the USA
Lexington, KY
27 September 2012